FROM: DADDY TO: DAUGHTER

The Secrets My Daughter Taught Me About Being A Great Dad

Anthony KaDarrell Thigpen
Amber Kindness Thigpen

FROM: DADDY TO: DAUGHTER

Published by Literacy in Motion
1901 W. Germann Rd.
Chandler, AZ 85286

Cover Photography by **Baylee Fetcher**

Anthony KaDarrell Thigpen editorial services, a subsidiary of Literacy in Motion.
Library of Congress Cataloging-in-Publication Data Publisher and Printing by Literacy in Motion Cover Design by Literacy in Motion Design Team

FROM: DADDY TO: DAUGHTER
ISBN: 978-0-9904440-9-1
Family
Self-Help Printed in the United States of America

TABLE OF CONTENT

Introduction

Daughter's Are Delicate Gifts From God

Daddy thank you for putting me first!

Love,
Amber Kindness Thigpen
Happy Father's Day

I used to think a great dad was merely a man who provided financially, invested quality time, and taught his children the necessary life lessons to achieve success. That remained my sole theory until I had my only daughter, Amber Kindness. While those things are essential, I now understand why texted book licenses aren't required to raise children. You see, the truth is, more than anything I've ever done for our daughter, her existence in my life has enhanced me beyond words. Our daughter is God's delicate gift to me. I've learned what it means to be a great dad by being present, being attentive, and being prayerful.

Mistakes are also a part of the process – learning and growing through challenges and difficulties as a family. Like everybody else, we have our good and bad experiences, but love and forgiveness is the theme of our home. *From: Daddy To: Daughter* is my most sincere heartfelt expression of how magical every moment is raising our precious little girl. It's a short-easy-to-read book that uniquely celebrates "Father's Day" everyday. Children need parents, both dads and moms, and despite the success of single-family structures, I'm grateful that our daughter is graced to grow up in the care of my wife and I.

As a dad, I learned everything I know about gentleness from our daughter. Her interactions and reactions made me realize I possessed the power to build her self-esteem, to strengthen her spiritually, to help her to live a healthy lifestyle, to insist that she focuses on high academic achievement, and to make her feel pretty.

The beauty of being a great father is that children don't care about how much money you have, or don't have. Over the past 10 years, Amber made me realize that children just want your undivided attention – and that doesn't cost a thing. Little girls want to hear you whisper, "You are so special." They want to feel protected emotionally. They want you to know that they can count on their dads. Most importantly, daughters want to know that their fathers are listening, even to the words that never come out of their mouths.

Daddy/Daughter Journal

Daddy/Daughter Journal

Daddy/Daughter Journal

Daddy/Daughter Journal

Daddy/Daughter Journal

Daddy/Daughter Journal

Daddy/Daughter Journal

Daddy/Daughter Journal

Daddy/Daughter Journal

Daddy/Daughter Journal

Chapter 1

The Art of Listening

Hearing What The Heart Is Saying

Thank you for making me cleanup my room. You make sure the house is clean before I come home from school!

Love,
Amber Kindness Thigpen
Happy Father's Day

Right from the beginning at birth, she taught me the importance of listening. I listened when she cried as a newborn. I listened to her underdeveloped baby talk. I put my fingers on her chest listened to her heartbeat while she was sleeping. Mostly, I listened to her facial expressions and emotions! I still listen. I studied her behaviors and learned the art of listening.

Listening is when you diligently try to comprehend, beyond words and body language, and despite emotions and personal beliefs. Listening has nothing to do with being understood, but understanding others.

Listening requires humility, because you must think of others as more importantly than oneself if you truly expect to hear what they are saying.

Listening is neither agreeing nor disagreeing, it is hearing the message behind the words, absorbing the content, and processing the conclusion.

Listening requires a level of consciousness and consideration about "why a person thinks and feels the way they do."

Listening demands support and affirmation without the need of reaction. Ineffective listening is waiting on a moment of silence so that you can get your personal point across.

Listening is an art form, because it is creating an atmosphere where individuals can trust that they are truly being heard.

There is no way to be a good listener if you don't practice positive thinking. I've seen so many parents lash out at their sons and daughters. As a result, cruelty becomes a part of their culture at an early age – and that's only the beginning the downward spiral. Cruelty cuts off her children's sentences, claims to know what his child is thinking, and cites language unsuitable for cultivating good character. This is why the next chapter is about positive thinking, because without it, it's quite difficult to break the cycle of negative results.

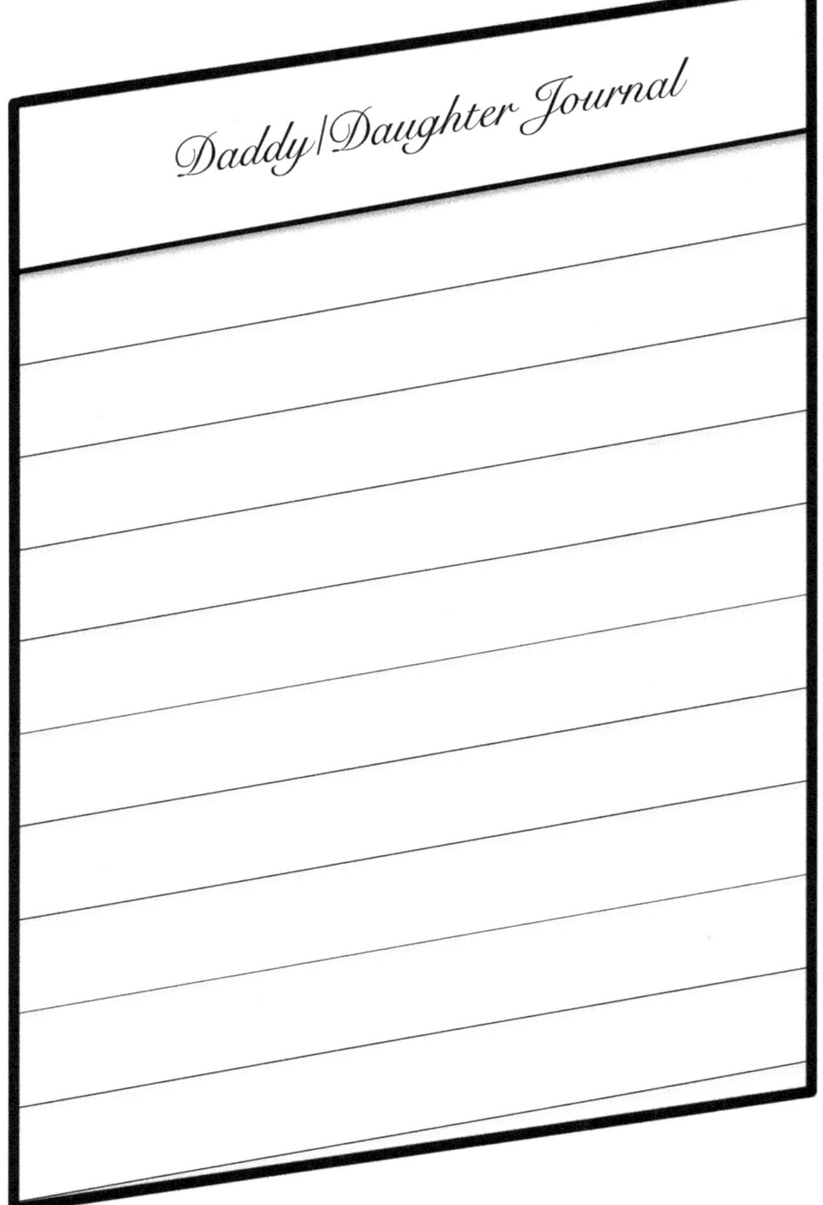
Daddy/Daughter Journal

Daddy/Daughter Journal

Daddy/Daughter Journal

Daddy/Daughter Journal

Daddy/Daughter Journal

Daddy/Daughter Journal

Daddy/Daughter Journal

Daddy/Daughter Journal

Daddy/Daughter Journal

Daddy/Daughter Journal

Chapter 2

Positive Thinking

Good Thoughts, Good Words, And Good Deeds

Thank you for Loving
me and taking care of me.

Love,
Amber Kindness Thigpen
Happy Father's Day

Amber taught me how to always maintain positive energy - at least to try anyway. As a result, my personal motto is "Thinking good thoughts, speaking good words, and doing good deeds". This is what I call "The 3-G Lifestyle".

All children are amazing, and daughters are amazingly delicate. We should all glean from their innocence, and make sacrifices to preserve it. Notice how children don't allow race, politics, religion, or economics to dictate their love, interaction, playtime, or forgiveness. They don't hold grudges, they call everybody on the playground their friends, and they look for inexpensive and creative way to show love. In part, this is what makes all children, especially daughters, and in particularly Amber, so peculiar.

Amber and I paint together, even though we're not artist. We sing, even though we can't hold a tune. We dance together, she's thinks I have rhythm, but that's not the same story you'd hear from my wife. The point is, who cares if you're not the best at anything. Just do a little of everything, because Amber taught me that daughters are just looking for a way to connect, smile, and have fun.

Fun is anything used to lighten the mood. Even just tickling your daughter can stir a sense of happiness, or for that matter wrestling with your son. Once the mood is lightened, the atmosphere is set for positive energy to flow freely. Afterward, good thoughts come naturally. Where there are good thoughts, good words and good deeds come hand-in-hand.

Emulating these characteristics has enriched my life. So, I've made it my purpose to think good thoughts even when bad things are happening. I choose to speak good words even I've been wronged. Most importantly, I've made it my habit to do good deeds daily. As a result, I touch the lives of strangers, and embrace the hearts of friends and family. The more good you do, the better you'll feel about life.

Good thoughts, good words and good deeds are my way of life as a dad. It's stress-free, rewarding and kid-friendly. By doing so, our daughter lets her guard down, she feels that she can trust the atmosphere I've created, and it shows in her behavior and body language. It's extremely important that our daughters feel like they are invited, welcomed, and valued in our presence as dads. This is dictate how they process every relationship they share in life. The 3-G Lifestyle promotes positive thinking that will enhance your fatherhood tremendously.

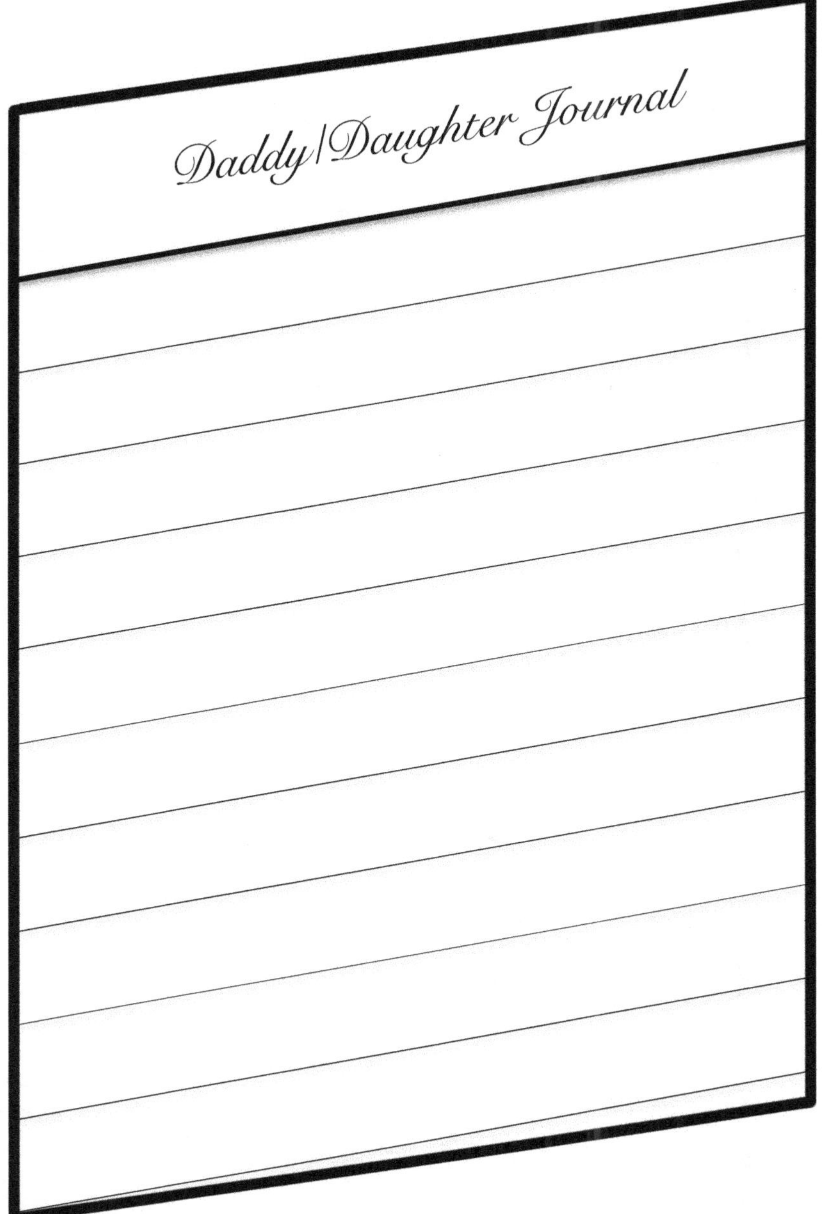
Daddy/Daughter Journal

Daddy/Daughter Journal

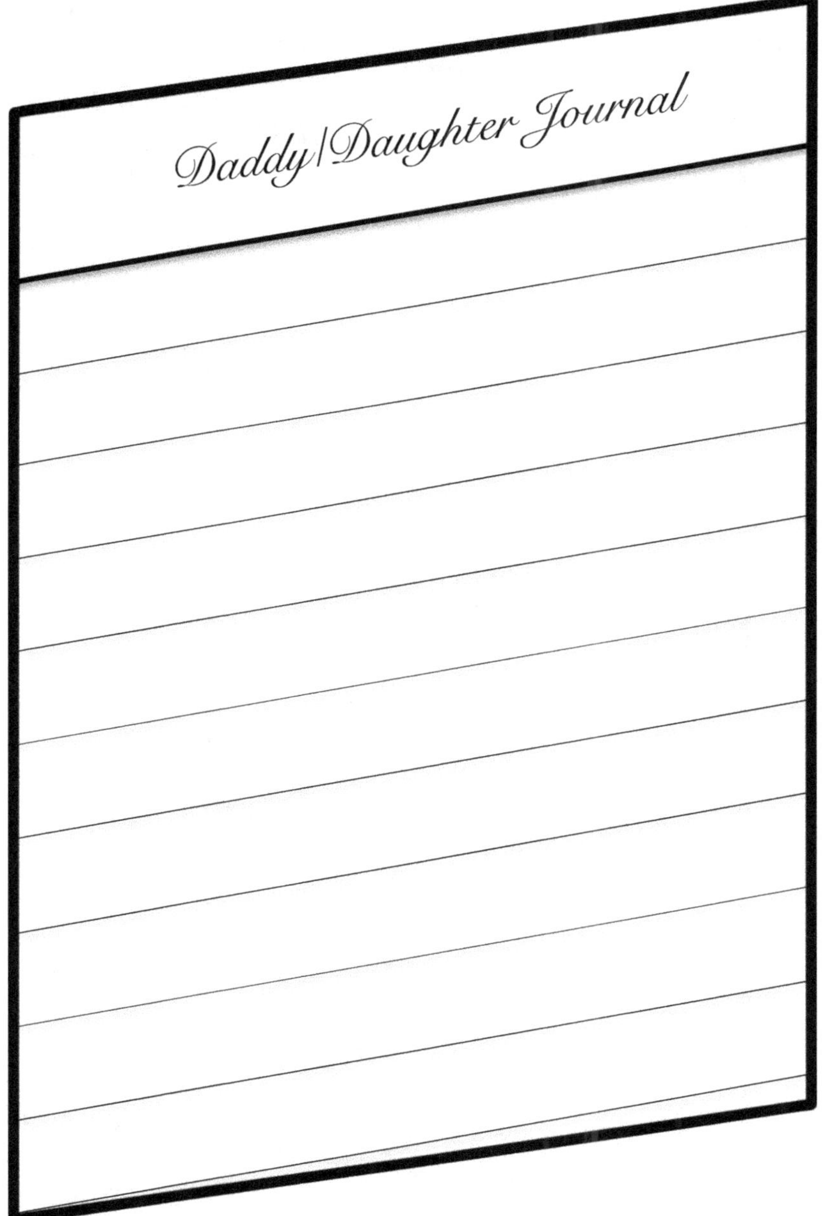
Daddy/Daughter Journal

Daddy/Daughter Journal

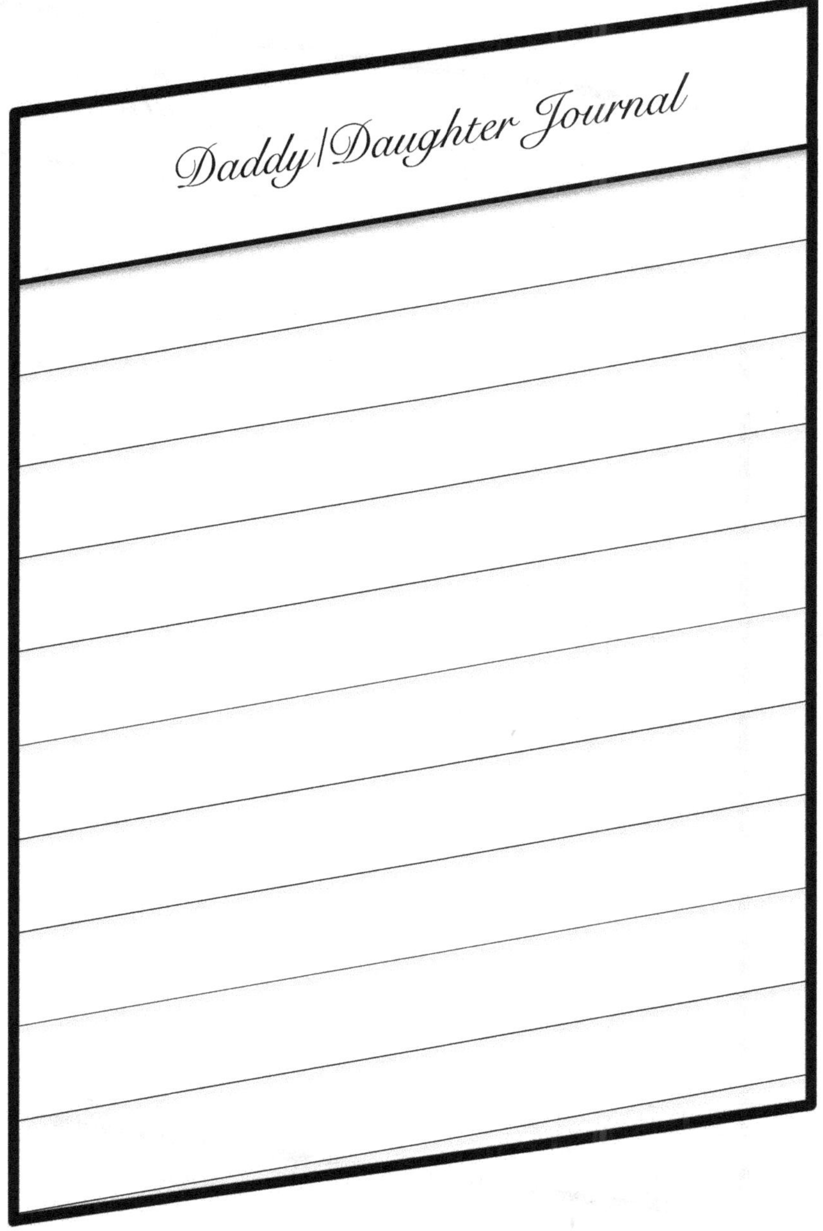
Daddy/Daughter Journal

Daddy/Daughter Journal

Daddy/Daughter Journal

Daddy/Daughter Journal

Daddy/Daughter Journal

Daddy/Daughter Journal

Chapter 3

Love & Selflessness

Giving The Gift Of Godliness

Daddy thank you for playing volleyball

Love,
Amber Kindness Thigpen
Happy Father's Day

Raising a daughter isn't always a combination of easy task, especially not as a dad, even with the help of mom. I've had to learn how to do things I never expected, like washing and styling hair and answering weird questions in creative ways – lots of weird questions. Truth is being a great dad has an awful lot to do with reprogramming the brain to focus on others before oneself. I've had to learn new academic and creative things that I had no interest in. I have to remain open minded. In essence, raising a daughter can be difficult at times, because the greatest lesson is learning that nothing is necessarily about you, as a dad. Being a great dad demands love and selflessness.

I admit, I'm very skeptical of many common feel-good aphorisms, and here's one at the top of my list, "You've got to love yourself before you can love anybody else." Truth is, my love for Amber daily diminishes the thought of "self love". And I'm okay with that, because the love she showers me with in return satisfies my selfish desire to "love myself." Any active parent will tell you, their child comes first, always and all the time. Good parents don't even entertain the idea of putting self first, it's simply not an option.

Parental love, as with any other expression of true love, requires selflessness. Hence, even the concept of "self" love is a contradiction because love is selfless. Amber, this is something I always want you to remember, because if you ever expect to experience true love, you have to be willing to give it. You have to realize that the reason love makes you vulnerable is because your heart will be at the mercy of others. Yes, of course you'll get hurt, possibly even damaged depending on the type of people you choose to love, but time heals. When you get older, read these words as a reminder during difficult times. Afterward, hold your head up and keep moving forward knowing that better days are always ahead.

Dads, young men are deceiving and manipulating our daughters because everybody has their own definition of what love is. I teach our daughter to stick with the biblical definition of love. The Bible does a remarkable job defining 16 characteristics of love. If a person says they love you, and their actions don't fit this description, then it's not love.

"Charity (1) suffereth long, and is (2) kind; charity (3) envieth not; charity (4) vaunteth not itself, (5) is not puffed up, (6) Doth not behave itself unseemly, (7) seeketh not her own, (8) is not easily provoked, (9) thinketh no evil; (10) Rejoiceth not in iniquity, but rejoiceth in the truth; (11) Beareth all things, (12) believeth all things, (13) hopeth all things, (14) endureth all things. Charity (15) never faileth: but whether there be prophecies, they shall fail; whether there be tongues, they shall cease; whether there be knowledge, it shall vanish away. ...And now abideth faith, hope, charity, these three; but (16) the greatest of these is charity" (I Corinthians 13:4-8, 13).

There is no better way of knowing if someone truly loves you or to exercise loving others then to put these 16 traits into practice everyday:

1. **Suffer long**
2. **Kindness**
3. **Absent of envy**
4. **Does not brag**
5. **Absent of arrogance**
6. **Does not dishonor others**
7. **Selflessness**
8. **Not easily angered**
9. **Keeps no records of wrongs**
10. **Delights not in evil, but rejoices in truth**
11. **Protects**
12. **Trust**
13. **Hopes**
14. **Perseveres**
15. **Never fails**
16. **Believes that there is nothing greater**

Obviously no one is perfect. As a dad, I want to put things in perspective so that in years to come our daughters will be able to keep a score card for the first 6 months of dating before making permanent relationship decisions. Consider the chart on the next page and valuate his ability to love you.

This works for friends, too. Love is not a feel-good emotion validated with all-night phone calls and goose bumps. Love is a decision, and you must always evaluate the quality of your relationships based on the word of God. I've created a comical but true example for you to follow. If you take heed, it's likely that it will avoid your future rescue and spare some lost soul from the wrath of your father.

GRADE YOUR RELATIONSHIP

Perfect Score	16 out of 16 = 100%	A+ (Marriage)
-1	15 out of 16 = 93.8%	A (Keeper)
-2	14 out of 16 = 87.5%	B+ (Commit)
-3	13 out of 16 = 81.3%	B- (Pray)
-4	12 out of 16 = 75%	C (Question)
-5	11 out of 16 = 68.8%	D (Withdraw)
-6	10 out of 16 = 62.5%	D- (Destruction)
-7	9 out of 16 = 56.3%	F (Torment)

(Score Sheet: I Corinthians 13:4-8, 13)

When we examine our lives, we must also consider our relationships. Our daughters have the most difficult time doing so. I hope this book helps more than just my own daughter, but perhaps my words will encourage other dads and countless young ladies. Love and selflessness does not mean lust and stupidity. All people deserve to experience true love, selflessness and kindness – never settle for less.

Amber's actions taught me that love is the kind of gift that we give to others, and sometimes we'll receive nothing in return. In a society where people selfishly put themselves first, selfishness reigns and individualism is the agenda of the day. Selfless love is costly and rare, but it's so beautiful and worth the sacrifice.

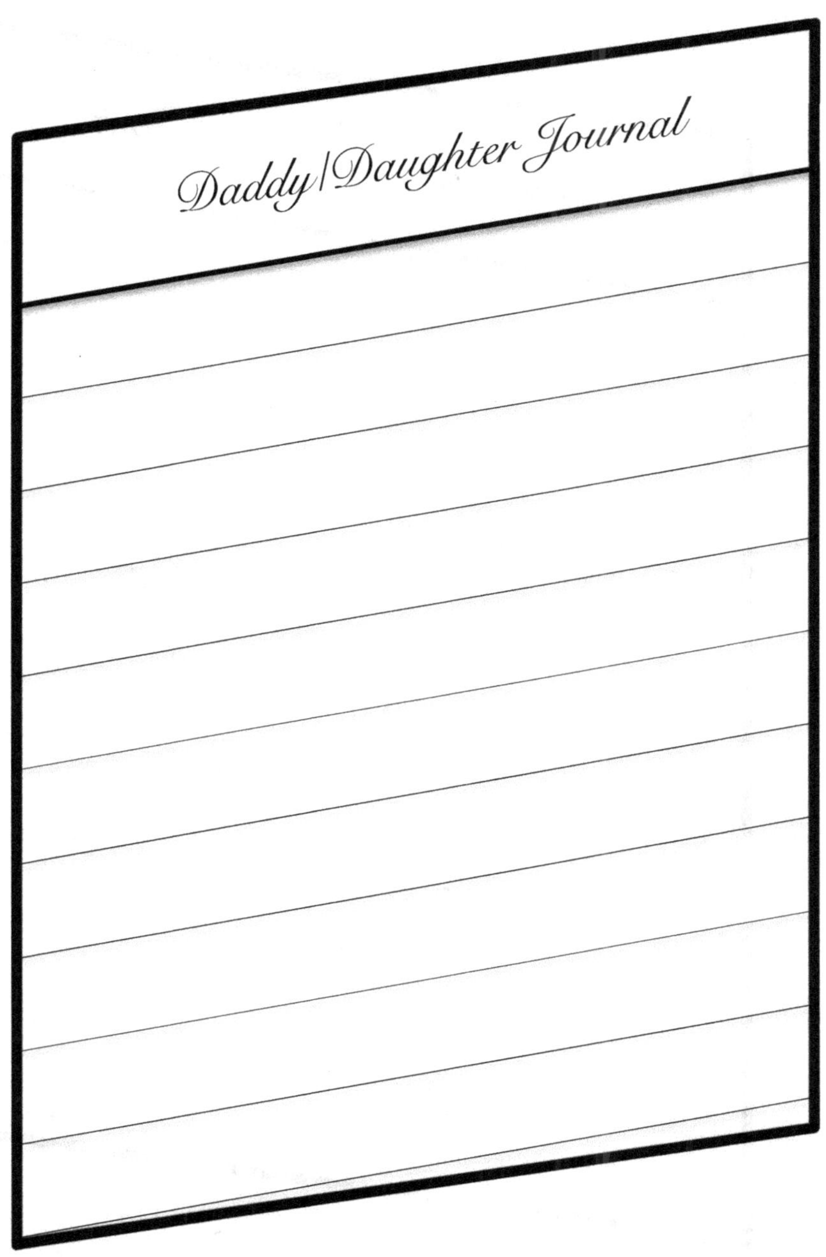
Daddy/Daughter Journal

Daddy/Daughter Journal

Daddy/Daughter Journal

Daddy/Daughter Journal

Daddy/Daughter Journal

Daddy/Daughter Journal

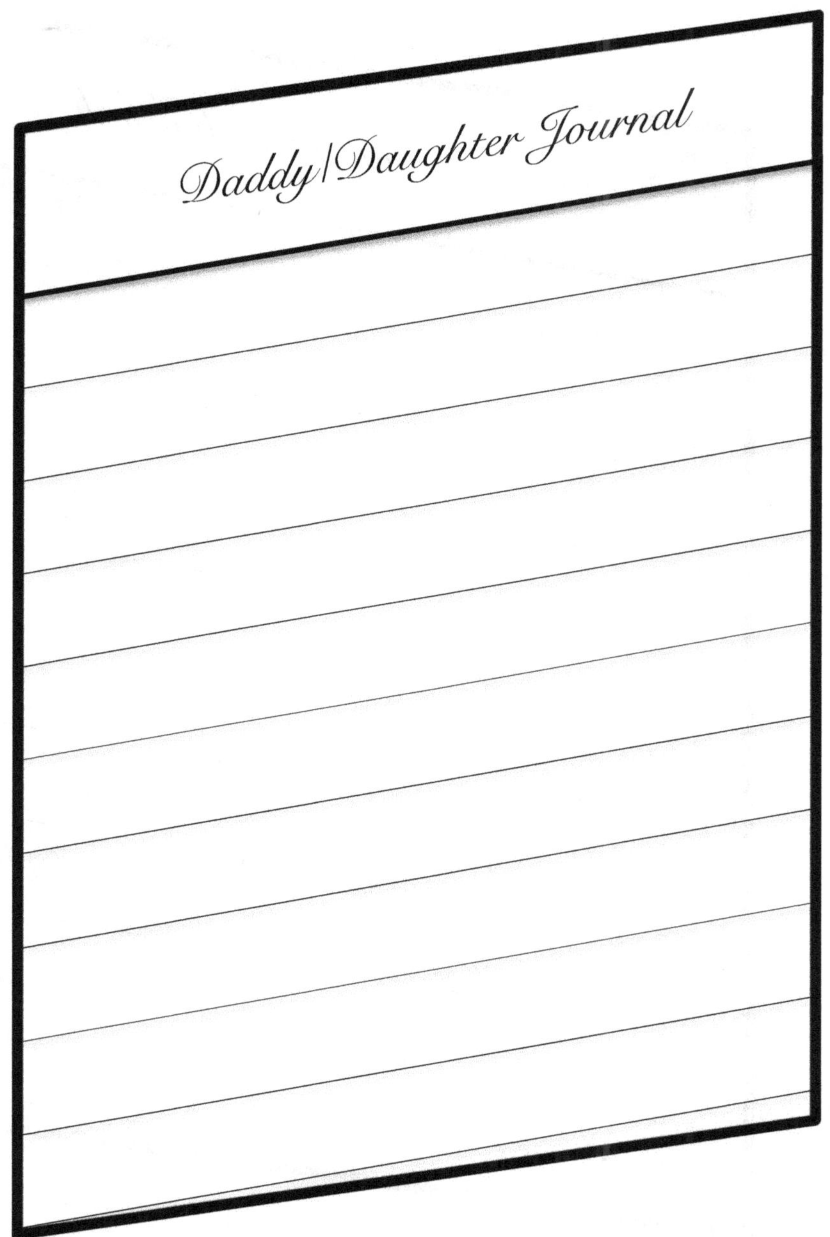
Daddy/Daughter Journal

Daddy/Daughter Journal

Daddy/Daughter Journal

Daddy/Daughter Journal

Chapter 4

Humility

Treating Humanity With Dignity

Thank you for surprising me
with cool gifts and places to go!
Thank you for making sure i have
something to do for my birthday!

Love,
Amber Kindness Thigpen
Happy Father's Day

Humility is one of the most difficult lessons I've learned from my 10-year-old daughter. Amber treats and thinks of others as though they are more important she. I used to have an issue with that. I was concerned about her being railroaded, mistreated, and misused. I now understand we cannot shelter nor isolate ourselves from humility in effort to avoid betrayals and injustices. Under no circumstances should human dignity be belittled – all people are important.

It is honorable to treat others as though they are more important than you. This does not take away from nor lessen our own dignity; it adds to our character. This is not a weakness; it is noble strength. I desperately hope that our daughter always remember that humility is the foundation of good character, good morals, and a good heart. A person who does not exercise humility will never truly love you. They will not consistently sacrifice for you. They will debase you as a friend. They will overlook the virtue of kindness and they will hear you speaking, but not listen to what your heart is saying. Daughter, humility is the main ingredient to everything described in this book.

It takes nobility, confidence and high self-esteem to treat others as though they are more important. Humility enables us to share the little we have to feed the poor; to respect people despite their failures; and to do things to remind people that they are greater than their mistakes and misfortunes. Humility prevents us from looking down on others. Where there is no humility you'll find segregation, arrogance, negativity, and everything else that divides the human race.

I started by treating and thinking of my family as thought they are more important. After seeing how empowering that was for my wife and daughter, I started treating others as though they are more important. Now, I aim to empower everyone I encounter the same way simple by being humble.

Everybody should know just how important he or she is, from children to adults. Humility is our assurance of making everybody feel equal, empowered, and esteemed. The birth, life, and personality of our daughter truly bring out the best in me. I only hope I can impart in her as remarkably as she's enlightened me. Amber, always remember, I am truly thankful that God gave you to me.

Daddy/Daughter Journal

Daddy/Daughter Journal

Daddy/Daughter Journal

Daddy/Daughter Journal

Daddy/Daughter Journal

Daddy/Daughter Journal

Daddy/Daughter Journal

Daddy/Daughter Journal

Daddy/Daughter Journal

Daddy/Daughter Journal

Chapter 5

Friendship

Sharing What's Pure In The Most Precious Way Possible

Thank you for doing my hair!
I really do like the way you wash,
condition, and rod my hair!

Love,
Amber Kindness Thigpen
Happy Father's Day

Amber calls me her best friend, and as her dad, I wear that badge proudly. I'm well capable of wearing multiple hats, from father and friend, to hairstylist and helping with homework, and from provider to preparing meals, being a great dad should never have limitations.

Every little girl would benefits from having her own dad as a best friend. This merely makes me the standard barrier for others in her life. Friendship amongst females can be filled with drama, ups and downs, gossip, and negativity. Daughters with active dads possess the ability to help their daughters think logically, as opposed to emotionally.

Our daughter is convinced that she will forever be my best friend. That doesn't necessarily sound realistic, but without question, I'll always be in her corner. While we share this incredible father/daughter relationship I'm using it as an opportunity to shape her opinions and expectations of friendship. The best way to determine quality friendship is to listen carefully to what people say and then you'll understand their true intentions.

A true friend loves like family. They accept you for who you are and forgive the wrongs you do. I had to teach our daughter that everybody is not your friend. Innocence can make you gullible sometimes, or at least naïve. As an innocent little girl, she used to think all classmates were friends. Likewise, some adults use the term freely and set themselves up for failure and disappointment. People will talk and tell you secrets for a variety of reasons, and these reasons do not always end with friendship being the motive. I can think of about 6 reasons why people pour their hearts out.

The first group is people that don't have anybody to confide. So, the vent to people they have no attachment to, using random people as sounding boards. Do not confuse this with friendship.

The second group can be dangerous. These people actually want you to believe that they are your friends, but actually they are only pretending to vent. Truth is they're using you has an emotional garbage can. Beware of negativity, regardless of how it's disguised.

The third group is much like the second, instead of merely polluting your spirit, they communicate with hopes of making you their puppet. They tell you only what they want you to know, leaving out key points, with the expectation that you'll react exactly how they want you to.

The fourth group is questionable. These are the people who tell you enough information just to get more information out of you. This person could be a genuine friend or maybe not, it all depends on the information being exchanged and how they plan to use.

The fifth group of people operates as true friends. They tell you secrets, details, and hold nothing back with the hopes that you will give them sound counsel and good advice.

The sixth group communicates on the level of the fifth, although they don't want advice or counsel, they need a peacemaker, someone to mediate on their behalf.

When people are talking to you, usually their stories, experiences, and dialog can be placed into one of these 6 categories. Instead of wondering why a person is telling you something, stop them. Afterward, simply ask, "Just so that I can follow you, first explain why are you telling me this?" This simple question, and little dose of advice will prevent so many heartaches and help you to avoid piles of drama.

This is helpful information for our daughters, because tweens and teens find themselves trapped within the maze of "He said she said." So for now, I'm teaching our daughter how to connect with positive people. In the meanwhile, I'll continue being her best friend, and we'll keep sharing what's pure in the most precious way possible.

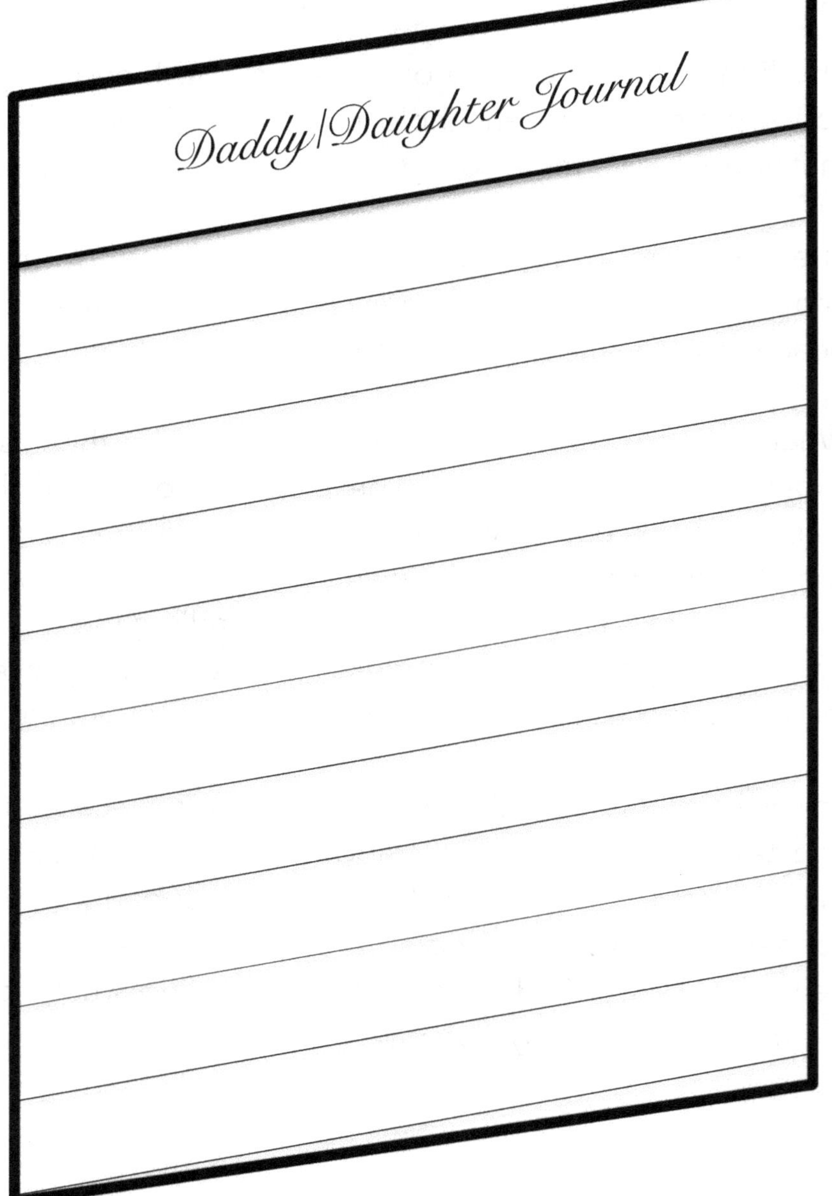
Daddy/Daughter Journal

Daddy/Daughter Journal

Daddy/Daughter Journal

Daddy/Daughter Journal

Daddy/Daughter Journal

Daddy/Daughter Journal

Daddy/Daughter Journal

Daddy/Daughter Journal

Daddy/Daughter Journal

Daddy/Daughter Journal

Chapter 6

Kindness

The Most Attractive Trait Anyone Has Ever Had

Thank you for Loving me and taking care of me.

Love,
Amber Kindness Thigpen
Happy Father's Day

I've saved the best for last. Our daughter's middle name is Kindness. She is truly one of the nicest people I know. According to the Bible, every believer connects with God based on one characteristic, loving-kindness (See: Jeremiah 31:3). We are attracted to kindness more than anything else. Amber, I want you to remember that kindness will enable you to connect with people.

Kindness doesn't cost you a thing. However, people don't owe you kindness so always return the gesture with gratitude. Kindness has more to do with the energy you give off than the deeds that you do – people can feel positivity. Kindness must become a part of your thought pattern before you start doing good deeds and speaking good words, otherwise you'll come across as self-righteous and self-gratifying.

On this Father's Day 2016, I am forever etching my words with yours. Writing is my greatest passion, and today, I give this gift to you. Thank you for all the kindness and gratitude you've given me. This is the shortest book I've ever written, but the most meaningful thoughts I've ever expressed. I hope my words meet you in your future, embrace you in my absence, and give you guidance in my silence. I am always with you.

Daddy/Daughter Journal

Daddy/Daughter Journal

Daddy/Daughter Journal

Daddy/Daughter Journal

Daddy/Daughter Journal

Daddy/Daughter Journal

Daddy/Daughter Journal

Daddy/Daughter Journal

Daddy/Daughter Journal

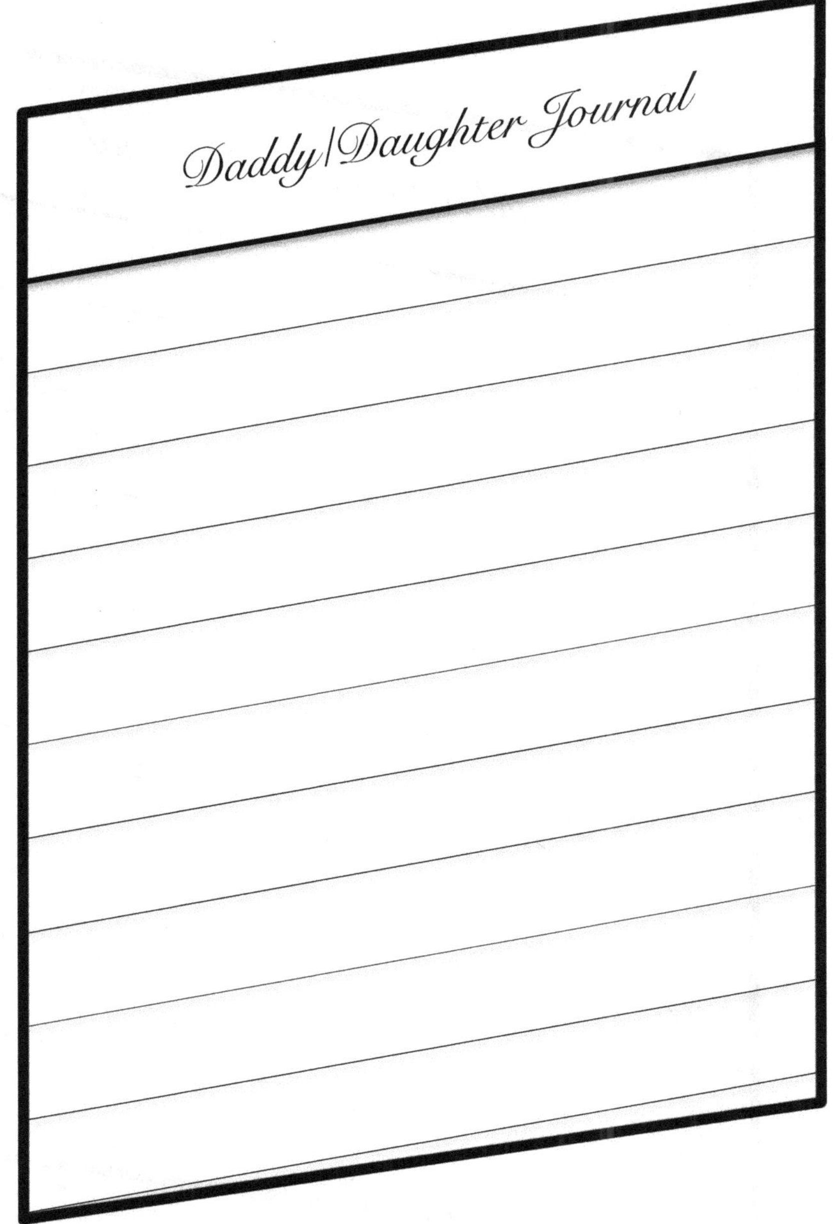
Daddy/Daughter Journal

Daddy/Daughter Journal

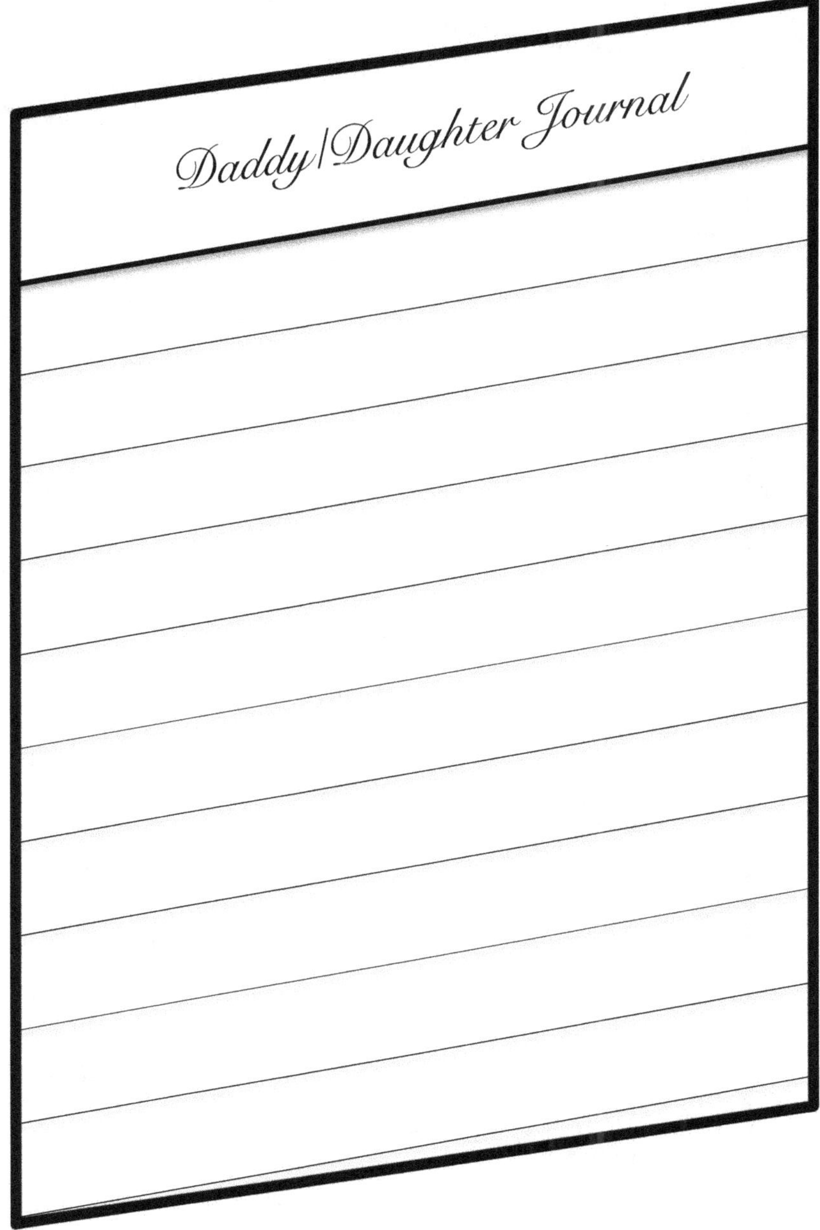
Daddy/Daughter Journal

Daddy/Daughter Journal

www.ingramcontent.com/pod-product-compliance
Lightning Source LLC
Chambersburg PA
CBHW070536030426
42337CB00016B/2224